NAVARASA - SOUL TIDES

LEKHASHREE NATARAJAN

Clever Fox®
PUBLISHING
Chennai • Bangalore

CLEVER FOX PUBLISHING
Chennai, India

Published by CLEVER FOX PUBLISHING 2026

ISBN: 978-93-7500-340-3

"Kinstugi teaches us that repair can be more beautiful than perfection ever was."

ACKNOWLEGEMENT

This book carries many hearts within it, but first and foremost, it carries my father's. To my dad, thank you for being my constant strength, my quiet reassurance, and my loudest cheer. Through every high and every trembling low, you have stood beside me with unwavering faith. Your love has been my shelter, your belief my courage, and your smile the gentle reminder that I could dream, fall, rise, and still be held. This book is as much yours as it is mine.

A special, deeply grateful thank you to John — my well-wisher, my steady support, and an unshakeable pillar through this journey. This book would not exist without you. Thank you for pushing me when I doubted myself, for guiding me when I felt lost, and for being there through every step, every word, every hesitation, and every breakthrough. Your encouragement lit the path when it felt dark, and your faith carried this dream forward.

This book is a celebration of Navarasa — of love and loss, courage and stillness, anger and grace, joy and sorrow, surprise and truth. It is a tapestry of emotions stitched together through poetry, reflecting the delicate and powerful journey of the human soul, just as dance has always taught me.

To everyone who has ever felt deeply, lived bravely, and allowed themselves to feel every shade of being human — this book is for you.

With gratitude and love.

A NOTE TO THE READERS

This book began long before the first word was written — it began on stage.

In the stillness before music, in the breath that holds a story, in the language of movement that my body learned before my pen ever did. As a classical dancer, Navarasa has always lived within me — the nine sacred emotions that shape expression, art, and the human soul. Over years of dancing them, I began to feel them not just as performance, but as life itself.

These poems rise from that journey.

They wander through love and loss, anger and courage, happiness and grief, wonder, disgust, and finally the gentle quiet of peace. Each rasa is a pulse of existence — sometimes trembling, sometimes fierce, always deeply human. What Bharatanatyam expresses through the body, these pages now express through words.

This is my first book, but it carries countless emotions lived, endured, cherished, and transformed. I offer it to you as a companion — for the days your heart feels heavy, for the moments your spirit feels brave, for the times you simply need to remember that you are alive and feeling.

May these poems hold your emotions the way dance once held mine.

May they remind you that every feeling has a purpose, every ache has a story, every silence has depth.

And may you always find your way back to peace, the still center after every storm.

Welcome to Navarasa.

Welcome to the many rhythms of being human.

CONTENTS

SHRINGARA (LOVE/BEAUTY/ ROMANCE)

1

QUEST

As the dusk went down for the dawn to rise,
I worried about the moon fading away into the glary glow,
prying for its return,
I asked the mighty celestial, where do you go?
The Moon responded,
As the sun descends to oblivion,
as darkness scatters its wings of triumph,
painting a masterpiece of its own mind,
with shades of gloom each eventide,
I patiently await,
for my turn to shine.
Embellished, for my lover boy.

2

REMINISCENCE

The faint thought of shells caressing on the seashore,
the subtle clinging in the face of the silver crests,
took me to the world where I was still your lady-love.
Etched to my heart was your broad-day like smile,
and alluring eyes,
where you and I were companions of the moon,
skinny dipping till dawn,
devouring each moment as it untwined,
burrowed in our long-lost tales,
Vowing eternal bonds.

Reminiscence slyly whispered in my ear at the moment
—
The unkindness of the truth
It pricked my numb heart as though it could feel again.

I picked up the loneliest shell
and gazed at the moon whilst sauntering away in solitude,
Wondering if your eyes still twinkle the same.

3

STARRY NIGHT

What would the night do without the sparkling stars,
that shine oh! so bright,
without any expectation.
The dead of night would feel naked and coy,
'cause It was never called the moony night.

It's the moody stellars that paint the heavens,
like the little things that make our lives.
And if you are not the moon to your lover,
dont be down-heartened.
The dark sphere can survive without its moon,
but is an unfinished art without the sprinklers of its fairy dust.
We chase the moon so much,
we neglect the mighty wink of the demigods.
Scarcity of the moon makes it special,
but on a moonless dusk,
It's the stars that breathe the space,
filling it with a beacon of radiance,
when it's most needed.
Always present,
twinkling in a far away cosmos.

4

I WILL WAIT FOR YOU

Even during the darkest days of my life,
I will wait for you,
with a prick in my heart,
becoming bigger and bigger,
like a piece of paper slowly burning,
unfurling till it turns into ashes.

And if we were in the eighteen hundreds,
you'd be like consumption,
spreading through my body
till my bones become brittle,
and blood sucked out
like I was bitten by a vampire.
You'd be my last hours of numbing ache,
That blazes through my hands and feet.
I'd be laying on my death bed
Becoming frail every passing moment,
with a miniscule hope of whatever remains
I have of you.
With my soul swifting away,
and your echoes fading slowly,

hovering somewhere around my rotten flesh.

And as I slowly reach my last gasp,
I'd close my eyes,
and my white pale body
will be a witness to the yearning of you.
And in that moment,
with my chapped lips,
I'd try to utter your name,
having a daymare of you holding my lifeless vein.

As I ingratiatingly smile,
For your approval to die.

5

YOU

You are the music in my heart and the champagne in my glass,
My morning sunshine and the ooze in my spine,
You are whispers of the waves and the magical realm I rave,
An enchantment's twin and the perfect sin,
You are the petrichor of the rain and drug to my melancholic strain,
My favourite excuse and adorned muse,
You are the tingling touch of the rainbow and the neon glow,
Precious triumph and my euphoric huffled puff,
You are the greens in my blunt and the shadow I'd confront,
Nucleus of my cell and a divine spell,
You are the raging fire and the art I admire,
Also tranquility of the breeze and the heavens I breathe,
You are a mysterious galaxy and my dark fantasy,
My sanity and insanity,
You are my sacred harmony and a soothing melody,
You are not just you and still you.
You are the universe to my multiverse.

KARUNA (SORROW/ COMPASSION)

6

THE MORE YOU DIG THE MORE IT HURTS

I heard you were happy,
With the person you left me stranded,
I was happy for you,
But I didn't want to know more.
If I've understood one thing,
It is not to spade through something
that is not meant to.

As the buried corpses,
breathlessly await to get a hold of your awakened soul,
to live through you once again.
And when this happens,
they casually take over your lively essence,
leaving you to dissolve.
And all there is left is your living corpse.

A garden only grows on watered soil,
digging through the roots would destroy its core.

7

WATERS OF THE PARADISE

When the nightingale enchanted the dusky breeze,
I often thought about you,
like your memory was etched to its singing.

As time travelled with its coarse tone,
I couldn't hear the psalms of solace nomore.
As if my ears were deafening
with your savage hostility.

So I took a dive into the deep-sea,
hoping to drown forever,
in a no man's station to feel free.
The land that once was home,
now felt like a place I didn't belong.

I'd go to the shore each eve hours,
hoping to be lost in the waves of harmony.
And go on a hunt to find myself
to come back to nothingness of the coast.

You'd made me feel so little,

that when the sun ascended one day,
I couldn't see my shadow.
It didn't sit quite right with me,
you were so high on wanting more,
that I ran out of cures to heal you.
I vehemently tried to win you over,
like the moon that pleases the sky.

Until one night there was no moon,
and when the nightingale sang sweet lullabies,
I was delighted by the symphony,
without your strenuous notion.

I rushed to the sea with no moonglade,
leaving footprints on the shore,
that would disappear anytime now,
becoming one with the waters of paradise.

8

TO LOVE LIKE A MOTHER

I loved him like a mother, he said.

She couldn't comprehend that statement.
Anticipating that very declaration,

Her lips
Trembled,
Trying to hold it together,
Her eyes
twinkled,
As her tears waited at the edge
of her lower lid,
waiting to flow.
And in a minute,
she started bawling.

Her hands held her skirt so tight,
the fringe of her floral skirt crumpled,
till it wrinkled like a tie-dye,
only the colour was still white.

What happened?

He gently asked,

She was so overwhelmed,
that her tongue felt lifeless,
unable to move
to utter a single word,
she layed there in silence,
still squeaking,
in nothing but only one thought
ruminating over and over,
How can someone who hasn't felt
the unconditional love of a mother,
Love like a mother?

9

MOVE ON

People say move on,
and at some point we do,
breathe a little more,
smile a little extra,
worry a little less,
but the glimpse of the memory brings it all in.
A sudden crick and the subtle skip of the heart beat,
pricking the wound until it feels numb,
we strive to feel like it's over,
while fighting it.
And that is a struggle you live through a million times.
And yet is unnoticed,
like it's over,
like it's okay.
It's the battle between letting go and letting in.
Where you toughen yourself enough,
to let the moment pass.

RAUDRA (ANGER/FURY)

10

HOW DO I KISS AGAIN?

All I was reminded of was,
your sickening touch and loutish tone;
Loathsome kisses that wounded my soul.
How do I kiss again?
When those strokes stained
strains of melancholy,
wondering what more could I have done —
to stop , to drop , to destroy.
From running on my mind in a loop,
the peril night,
the silent sky,
Violent screams and a frightened heart.
Feelings mixed up in a palette,
the only color being gray,
Shady and stray,
haunting like a ghost,
from inside the picture.
How do I sleep tonight?
For this memory doesn't blackout,
for this remains a dark mark,
for it is deceased,
but alive at its thought.

11

WHO GAVE YOU THE RIGHT?

Who gave you the right?
To feel like you are in control?
My darling, don't you know?
Don't you know, to control another human is a myth?
To beat, to cheat, to gorge like I am a piece of meat,
to agonize my mane in the bustling street,
to patronize me till I started to believe.

Who gave you the right?
To harass your lady-love with passion oh! so barbarous,
to exploit someone's softness to distortion,
to smite, to strike, till my body turned black and blue.

A savage breed, a heinous creed.
We are all victims of our instincts,
but yours, my lover,
yours is a metaphor of tyranny.

Who gave you the right?
To think it's okay to torment a person's being,
oblivious to remorse, mindless of mortification,

to get away with the countless encounters of pure cruelty,
to bash my crown to the edge of the wall?

As I wiped the stains of your inhumanity
from the wall that bled with me,
I asked myself,
Where does so much hostility come from?

And now, as you lay on the wet floor,
on the stage of your stolen liberty,
I imagine you behind the pillars of justice.
I wonder if I gave you the right to be so destructive;
I questioned myself time and again,
ripping you off of your ruthless emancipation,
now my beloved, is the time I finally set myself free.

12

STAIN

Years of curses, years of pain
Who is to wash away the stain?

A stain that was given to you,
by the impression of a few.

A scapegoat, a labelled whore,
oh! there's always more.

Like being "her" is a sin,
Adding much to the chagrin.

Their filthy thought, their stone heart,
frequents itself with a drugged dart,
scars of poke fill your soul,
leaving no space for your role.

The stain, the shame,
it's not yours to tame!

You still scrub and rub till clean,
When you should be bleaching.

You give up, you fight,
tired of the spite,
it's their brains
that need some reasoning,
not your body,
not your garb.

13

THE BIRD THAT UNCAGED THE TRUTH

I went above and beyond for you,
trying to flee a cage I built for myself,
I mutilated my wings trying to get out,
hoping you'd be there to catch when I fall.
At first,
I thought I was seeking freedom —
freedom to have unconfined boundaries,
with you and my burdened self.
Once I got out the cage,
Damaged,
I realised I wasn't fulfilling my desire,
but yours.
For you to hold my harmless wings,
And see me agonize my existence.
I was just a play toy to you,
where I swayed to your pleasures,
till I couldn't anymore.

But for me —
It was my whole life,
wanting to leave that cage,
for my unsatiated self of your longing.
Now I can't help myself but wonder,
if being caged was imprisonment,
or to have been vandalized by you.
So now I gather my fallen feathers,
dip them in my blood, and try to write words.
Seeking to mend something that was not broken by me.
Wondering,
If my guarded cage was ever to be found by you?

14

JUST FOR A LITTLE WHILE

I thought my scars meant something,
for I am a survivor.
And when I was naked,
you would kiss all of them,
One by one,
Inch by inch,
to show me you loved me,
with my age old stains.
Some fresh, some buried,
but they were just a way of stalling,
in the name of shielding my petrified nerve.
Little did you know,
that they can't be scraped off like dirt;
it was just a way to make you feel whole.
As you bore your own scars,
for you to not feel alone.
Just for a li'l while.

HASYA (LAUGHTER/ HAPPINESS)

15

MY LIFE'S SYMPHONY

I wasn't meant to live this fast life,
I was made for slow mornings,
and subtle delights;

to feel the ordinary,
without rushing to chase yet another horizon;
treasure each fleeting moment,
and laughing our hearts out;

plant orchids in my little garden,
and wait for spring to arrive;
put my scarlet dress on,
without having to get to somewhere in haste;

make a cup of coffee,
and relish its faint bitterness;
look at the sky and breathe heavens,
like I learnt to breathe for the first time;

whisper sweet nothings in your ears,
while we lay on the bed,

and stare at the ceiling,
like the roof was wide open for us to picture the cosmic galaxies.

Be grateful of things sought and not,
write letters of love, life, hope and loss;
feel the merry in my heart,
like it was meant to coexist.
Not bothered —
about where it's going to fall apart.

Drag you to dance half-naked,
to the lyrics of the shifting breeze,
and watch movies till we fall asleep.

If I had a choice I would choose a color palette for our life,
of muted pastels and earthy tones;
Perch on the counter while you make
glaced pancakes,
holding a can of whipped cream,
waiting slyly to spray you,
so we could pretend to wash ourselves,
while we drown into each other,
and make love like the world was ending.

Open a bottle of wine,
and gaze at the half moon,
through the window

and hum honeyed melodies.
Glide our hands to the tune,
while we embrace every speck
of the lasting dawn.

To be completely consumed by it.

16

NOSTALGIA

I have a thing for old memories,
I love how they craftily get to you out of nowhere,
ushering us to moments
that are tucked deep in our fumbled heads.
The scent of a candle,
that faded denim you'd wear everywhere,
the design of a carpet, or a linen,
the colour of a wall that takes us to our childhood,
the smell of hot samosas that echoes a certain reminiscence,
a song that escorts us to a special face,
the baby blanket that we never could let go of.

It's so sudden,
it touches us like a gentle breeze —
Calm, cozy and soothing.
It doesn't happen each day,
but when it tingles our memory,
We feel the nostalgic brimming.
A time where we were wholly present.

The aroma of old books,
flipping through those pages

just to find an old pressed flower;
the touch of my mother's old saree,
that reminds me of her affectionate shrug;
The elephant plushie without which,
I wouldn't get through a night;
The blacks and yellows bustling through the city lights,
that I would watch through the windowsill;
The old lamp that still lingers somewhere,
flickering in the corner,
broken and faulty;
Yet we don't just get rid of these masterpieces.
'Cause a part of our lives still exists through it.
I remember I used to collect
chocolate wrappers as if it was luxury,
the sea shells that were painted in shades of the earth,
taken home as a souvenir;
the handwritten letters
that had stamps of different places,
neatly arranged in an age old box.

We always yearn for something old
that once belonged to us,
that kept us going,
dawdling through the years,
as we grew into many versions of us.

One fine afternoon,
when I was dwindling into nothingness,
I stumbled upon those vintage albums,

with flares on the photos,
taking me back to places I never could get to again.
And those pictures,
overwhelmed my soul and I could feel again,
It felt like a hug that I never got.
Those are the moments that can't be lived twice,
but can almost be felt in its purest essence.
We live for those smallest of moments,
trying to make peace with our everyday puzzles,
and with these tinkerbell jiffies,
we lighten up our hearts.
As humans,
we tend to forget the past,
or dwell on the adversity,
but these little things make up for it.
In a way,
We never can.

17

BITTERSWEET

I had a dream of you.
Cotton balls and a luminous star,
You and I, wandering hand in hand,
in a meadow full of wildflowers.
You plucked a bunch for me,
and I recieved it with a heart full of bliss,
with a sparkling smile on my face
— the smile you fell in love with.
Grateful for you,
grateful for your existence.

And I awaken,
with sweaty palms and shivers,
anguish and agony,
decorated on my bed-side,
as if it were a piece of ornament;
with a burning body and soul full of desire,
to live that very fantasy.

The sun was shy with a silver lining sky,
here you were with a wistful smile,
lingering on an old aged wood,
with a bunch of wildflowers in your hands,
reminding me that bliss is plausible even on death bed.

18

LOVE STORY

In a dim lit space,
bursting with laughter,
dazed with potion,
And hisses of smoke.
In a room full of eyes,
met the sight of two
strangers in the night.

With glimpses of silence,
amongst the mayhem,
was ineffable stillness,
and in that calm,
They became ONE.
And in that moment,
everything was forgotten,
like an enchanted spell.
The spirits shared
the same tongue,
Hand in hand,
whirling in the twilight,
embracing the touch
with a soft subtle kiss.

And they knew,
a story was ready to be lived,
souls waiting to be seen,
and it was the beginning ,
and the end.
Oh! love is a wicked game.

VEERA (COURAGE/ HEROISM)

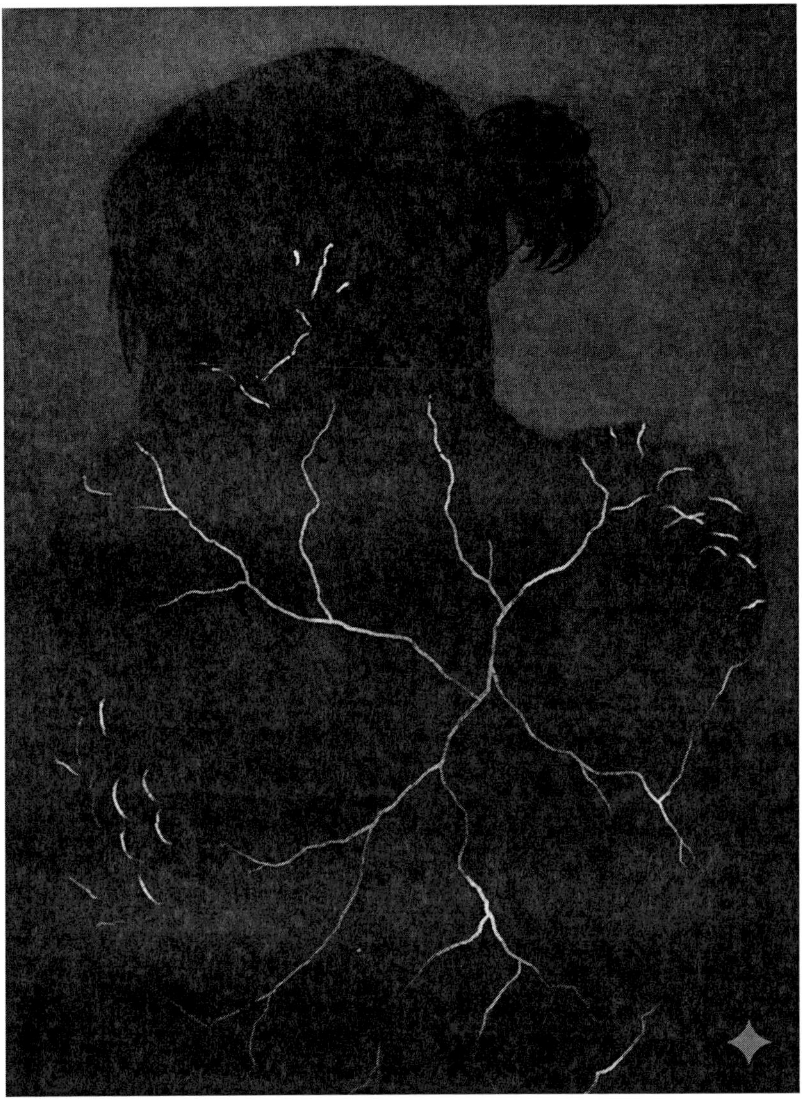

19

A WOMAN

She's beauty,
She's art,
Every wreck she departs.
She's the Goddess who births life,
Even the Gods cannot deny.
She's powerful yet mellow,
A tinge of elegance to her glow.
She's the form of discrete nature,
Every shape, size and colour is a creation.
She's a wonder to embrace,
Not a social disgrace.
And what does she receive?
Name, shame and defame
In forms colder than the shivers,
Frozen bitter for the giver.
Violence is the play they chose,
To harass, to assault, to abuse on the oppose.
Life turns into a nightmare,
For she's forever scarred.
Embedded deep in her skin,
The disgust, the filth, the sin.
Bearing the stain to her deathbed,
She passes with a punctured soul in her head.

When a woman says no, it's a no.

It's her choice, not a mold.
It's her right, not easily sold.
It's her body, not your gold.

20

WOULD YOU DARE IT?

Contradictory,
is the word.
As I wonder who I am?
Am I the fragile, sensitive, soft girl,
Or the bold, brave, confident woman?
I have a perception of myself,
And the world —
Oh! the world has views of its own.
But I own them differently,
in accordance with the circumstance.
So who am I?
If I tell you what I am made of,
the scars, the suffering, the pain, the rot,
would you still hear my story?
or walk away in between.
If I'd explain my roots,
would you see why some branches bear no fruit,
or reject me for my imperfection?
Would my distortion be repulsive to you,
or you'd see it as an abstract art?
If I rip off my skin and bones,

to show you my inmost fury,
would you fear my flaming rage,
or sit by my side as I stitch them with aurum?
If I bring out the little girl in me,
would you dismiss me for my childlike nature,
or ride the play-horse with me?

Who I am is a myth for many.
But to you I would reveal,
so would you be intrigued when I unviel my disguise,
or turn away as you don't have it in you to bear it?
To dare it.

21

THE LAST TOUCH

We talk about first love
like it's "my precious."
For the goblin it was.
Unlike the ring that demands greed,
this kind of love
is Santa's gift,
pure and innocent.
Affection so tender,
that tingles our stomach,
the first times,
too good to be true,
making it mystical.

When I fell in love for the first time,
I clung to it like it is my last,
that's what I was taught,
that love happens once.

But you and I —
you and I are different.
Probing for that warmth in our firsts, seconds,

maybe even our thirds,
yet somehow it didn't seem to transpire,
the very essentials that make you want ---
Or wanted.
With you,
when life is not an easy boat,
that's a risk I am not afraid to take,
with our fluctuating rhythms,
shimmying to our hymns,
writing our own li'l story.
All I wish,
is to be your last.
And you,
mine.
I hope for all my remains with you,
even the deadly inaugurals
of our unfinished record.
And one day,
When we'd have become so tight and entwined,
I'd have forgotten —
the rest of my former bygones,
for you'd have bestowed upon me,
the eternal tie of my pledged heart,
touching me for the very last time.

22

WHAT IS LOVE?

I was startled in the beginning,
aimlessly crouching over what love is?
Struggling to stretch
my being
as hard as I could
for your foreseen predictions.

I ran in circles,
refusing to believe it was a trap!

I believed I had to perform
in order to be loved,
I was convinced
that it was for the lucky ones,
the ones who demanded it,
the ones who deserved it.

It took me years of wreckage,
for me to let go of the race.
My spirit had slowed down,
I started to jog,
I walked,
then I stood still.

In the wake of the moment —
I shut down,
like the ruins of an old castle.

I was dumbstruck,
when the fallen leaves,
rose above
to craft a new being.
Like I could pull strings,
as though I had supernatural finesse.
Picking out the thorns,
one by one,
deeply embedded
in my body,
in my flesh;
deep in my bones.

I wouldn't lie to you,
it hurt
But I could now stand again.
I had broken my bones
just to mend it with gold —
Like kinstugi,
Lustrous and supreme.
It was tedious,
but I became wiser,
for I had stopped trusting
the wizard of my Beelzebub.
I confided in myself,

the roots of the hollow land,
that I had dug for myself.

Slowly, I had attained love,
by planting my own seed in the garden.

BHAYANAKA (FEAR/TERROR)

23

FEAR HAS TAKEN UP THE MOST SPACE

I feared all my life,

Of things, of people, of decisions, of opinions,
of everything I ought not to.

It scrutinized my soul so hard,
it started to feel familiar;
I juggled the same dysphoric illusion —
Of life, of love, of lust, of loss.

That the insides of me ground the gore
of the wickedness like it was natural.

Potential gone barren,
impressions turned into debris,
times squandered to absurdity.

My body turned blue, and heart —
Oh! my soulful heart,
became the possession I had to endure.
Sulking its existence,

wondering if I am a coward,
or just foolish, or crazy.
Worthlessness drove me to madness.
And with that madness,

I feared more.

Even when I had nothing to lose,
I still feared,
Out of all the things that spiral inside my ominous head,
Fear has taken up the most space.

Dark and sinister.

24

A TALE I WOULDN'T DARE TO SUMMON

I was once told a story,
Of a he and a she,
by two extremists,
Of love and war,
contradictions that intertwined.

I held on to the thought,
juggling,
I was bewildered,
with the two versions.
Wondering how?

One was of utmost tenderness;
Another of a raging ire,
One said it conquered all;
Another spoke of the void.

Creativity and destruction,
coexisted as a duo.
One was a ballad,

the other, an elegy.
Utter Silence and defeaning noise,
Walking hand in hand,
like they were the —
best of bosom friends.

Towards the end,
The only paramount,
was togetherness.
Of fire and ice
Blaze that dimmed,
Frost that melted,
In tandem,
striving to unite,
like a pandora's box
being unlocked.
The lack of certainty killed me,
but for the two it merged
them into One.
A tale I'd never dare to summon!

25

FEAR OF BECOMING SOMEONE ELSE

What's your biggest fear?
Someone asked,
Do you fear ghosts, goblins or thunder?
What's the one thing that scares you the most?
I sat there introspecting the question.
Is it my own demons that valour in my head,
Or that I would die anytime now?
Is it the paranormal creatures from the horror movies,
Or the ones I imagine under my bed?
Is it my fear of being unworthy of love,
Or not being enough?
Is it the fear of losing my loved ones,
Or an illness, there's no escape from?
Is it my 3 am thoughts,
Or my fear of heights?

What could possibly be my biggest fear,
I thought and thought —
To find out something very intriguing.
It's not the phantoms,
or the shadows,

or the devil,
that I fear the most,
It's my existence!
To experience life like it's mine ---
To make mistakes, to learn, to relearn,
to be happy, to be sad in my own skin,
To own my flaws and wins.
There is a way of the world,
I'd want to make my way in this world.
To be my soul-self, embracing patiently,
each eventide, as I wait for the next dawn to rise.

My biggest fear is the fear of becoming someone else,
I replied.

BIBHASTA (DISGUST/ AVERSION)

26

UNFAITHFUL FOREPLAY

We talked without the existence of time and space,
not bothered about the punctual pace.
We dragged our days and nights,
like tomorrow is a spite.
Floating through boulevard streets,
ready to sink in a heartbeat.
An aisle of cherry blossoms lined away,
as if it were our intended pathway.
We escorted the untrodden parade,
You and I, an unmasked charade!
Your edges soon chafed my tender gaze,
'cause to you, I was just a predictable maze.
The gentle breeze spun the tales of blare,
genesis of the hurricane naire.
My love was but a prolonged symphony —
of fondness, faith and flawful euphony.
Flaring fireworks of deceit and sophistry,
you stood there holding your pseudo chivalry.
I placed your unkind treacherous flowers,
in an ancient porcelain vase of the midnight hours.
Uncertain of your unpleasant spectacle,

I laid a bed of thorned roses far more cynical.
As I delved deep into a slumber soiree,
I fantasized your unfaithful foreplay!

27

TIRED

I am tired,
I am tired of your eyes perching my bosom,
I am tired of your lustful diligence,
I am tired of being an object, a subject, a concept,
I am tired of being fooled like it's so easy,
I am tired of seeming inviting for your mindless pleasures,
I am tired of you preying on my heart,
Like a starving vulture waiting to peck,
I am tired of yearning something real,
I am tired of your gilded palter,
I am tired of letting myself doubt my very nature,
I am tired of your pointless selfishness,
I am tired of the obscure impression you have of my desires,
I am tired of your deficient portray of my feminity,
I am tired,
but I am not giving up.
And I will not let this tiredness turn me cold,
I will not bear it to change it,
to escape your ruthless accusations.
I will not let myself drown in the image you have of me,

I will not let you bury my authenticity for your fetish,
I will not be the scratch to your itch,
I will be kind and give myself a chance,
if not it would be injustice —
Injustice to my fellow maidens and me,
I will be me and not what you want me to be,
For I will not let you soar with your sickening pier.

28

AN ELEGY TO THE MATRYRS

I found myself guilty to drown in my own sorrow,
to crack open a bubble of agony,
Sinful 'cause I had not been slaughtered
like the thousands of offsprings,
stripped off of their adolescence,
fighting a war they did not start,
Holding on to nothing but their loved ones,
only to find them a corpse the next morning.

I was bothered by my ignorance,
while the families starved to death,
enduring pain like it's a hobby,
lying there like somebody's watching,
till their last breath signaled a relief
And their memories wiped off.

I found myself regretting my pillows tears,
Wishing I had wiped them off
before it turned into a cloud.
When those helpless souls bustled to have a roof for the night.

aimlessly treading under the scorching sun,
To be the martyrs of the battle they never sought.

I was bothered by my disheartened life.
Wondering if I ever will be able to feel
my grief-strucken heart wholly.
Wondering if my melancholic strain will ever be enough
to wash away the stains of injustice?

ADBHUTA (WONDER/ AMAZE)

29

AN UNEXPECTED ENCOUNTER

I can't get over how familiar it sensed,
the longing in your sight,
and the throbbing of your spirit,
I am sure if we cut open our bodies,
we'd bleed the same tint.
As though we bore the same cruelty of life,
in ways only you and I recognize,
compassionate enough to let go.

Though I have met many of them,
I've never quite encountered anyone like you,
your eyes that spoke tales of within,
your hair that danced to your gestures,
laugh so innocent almost like it's pure.
Emotions so tender yet fierce,
like a divine intervention.

My contaminated heart felt unbound,
even though it was for a little while,
reminding me of my direction
to the love that sorcerizes souls.

We laughed amidst the mayhem of life,
filling it with soft silences,
arms brushing sweet strokes of ecstasy,
our cores intertwining into one being.
We took a promenade through the still city,
lusting a spell to capture our occasion,
we sat under the tree that gave life,
to the surreal beginning of the end.
Night was high,
And the hours stopped,
making space for us,
within the shadows of the dryad.

When we left I am sure a leaf tumbled as though it was fall,
in admiration of what we could have become.
Even though I sing symphonies of your absence,
You dwell in me through my poetic grace.

30

AS A CHILD I COULDN'T SPEAK

As a child I couldn't speak,
I'd stutter and mutter and swallow my words.
Nobody taught me to be not embarrassed —
I hid, I cried and ceased to rise.
So I didn't speak at all, even though at one point I could,
I spoke in my head and resisted any conversation.
And when I met people I didn't know,
I pretended to be confident in my speech.

Till one day,
When I realised I don't have to pretend anymore,
keeping in mind that I'd stutter anytime again,
but that didn't stop me from speaking.

And then I started writing,
I didn't have to worry about stuttering anymore,
I found my way to be able to spread my joyous wings.

31

NOTHING IS CONSTANT

And when the night comes crawling,
I sit on my creaking wooden chair with my naked soul in my hand.
Rocking questions of every life choice I've ever made,
Everything in and out,
I wonder what could have gone right,
My heart is heavy, and my life so light,
it could fly away with the softest blow of a child.
I enjoy the misery in solitude whilst knowing nothing is constant.

32

THE BIG OL' BOULDER

The wagon was moving fast,
and the wind was brushing strokes
of chillness on my face,
making it almost numb.
The wood of the Gods
adorned sprinkles of ice,
forming snow crystals.
I was wearing your hoodie,
the dusty blue one that I loved.

As I gazed to witness the stunning view,
one smoke streaked boulder
on the way looked at me,
like I was so small,
and our story even smaller —
We fought, we cried,
we compromised, we were fine,
It was our thing.
We were just two little wayfarers,
drifting through
the sublime nature of the roadway,

listening to our songs,
soaring high pitches.
We talked the fortune of our love,
like nothing else mattered.
As if it was only the two of us,
In this present time.

I couldn't stop thinking of the boulder,
that had crossed more than three miles away,
and the thought that it brought.
And if we had stopped there,
what stories it might have had to tell,
and how you and I,
would have our own comprehension,
nevertheless the boulder's.
In that moment,
I felt something.

Life in itself has innumerable realities,
a story is never the same,
it has its own veins.
Our existence has its own echoes,
chameleonic but ours,
passing like the clouds that are never still.
My narrative was mine and so was yours.
And the big old boulder's,
with its spars with the wind,
or just that it's bigger and bolder.

SHANTA (PEACE/ TRANQUILITY)

33

ALL, TO PASS

Life is created knowing there is death,
there is a beginning and an end,
the journey full of emotions that tend,
to caress and suppress,
with wonders of real or reel.
Goes on and on a cycle,
till this mortal existence's desire is fulfilled.
All, To pass.

34

AMATEUR

Life as a labyrinth,
I trailed through the hurdles and the aids,
the highs and the lows,
the rocky roads and the idyllic routes,
From zeroes;
through pseudo pores —
I escaped, I faced, I bent, I tripped, I walked straight.

Hope being my generous companion,
I held its string as vehemently as I could.
Even when I couldn't,
when my palms blistered,
when my demons whispered the wrath of defeat,
I stayed.
I stayed a mess,
I stayed with the horror,
I stayed when existing felt worthless,
I stayed when I had nothing to offer,

Do not mistake me to be brave,
I am just a girl learning to re-learn,

A tangled yarn, spinning through the maze,
Dwindling my desires, becoming small —
so small I could be invisible anytime now.

And then,

I paused.

To take a breath as my heart bled,
healing my core, curing my wounds,
touching my scars, reminding my intent.

I hit the dead end,
not once, not twice,
but a great many times.
Crawling,
gasping;
breathing,
reviving.

Lost but found, found but lost.

I found delight,
somewhere in between those walls,
of ebb and flow,
of distress and triumph,
of love and anger,
Of each encounter in its fullest form.

Today, Life is still a labyrinth,
but here I am welcoming it with open arms,
to greet it with fondness,
keeping fear in a far away land.

To accept, to live, to mold, to grow.
I learnt to experience living through it all,
and in doing so, I became alive.

Still being an amateur.

35

A LETTER TO MY MOTHER

It was a random sunday afternoon,
and I was laying on my off gray rug
in the TV room,
like I had an existential crisis.
Sun beaming on my placid face,
through the gaps of the window sill;
an unwatered plant and a glass of unfinished wine,
resting around like it meant something.
Staring at the ceiling that was once purple but now is white,
I look at the creaking fan,
a twirling piece of mechanic,
overwhelmed by its ordinariness.

I was reminded of our ballad,
the standard mother-daughter duo,
from once when I was your forsaken daughter.

I pondered, fidgeting on the pale floor,
how days turned into months, and months into years,
swifting as if it was fulfilling its purpose,

quietly existing as many moons passed,
I grew up somewhere in between being your offspring,
and becoming my own self.
Learning and unlearning,
worn between feeling too much and not feeling enough.

I shrunk my essence that was glued to you,
so much so that, its existence begun to feel like a myth.
I would watch movies all night,
and when the clock struck three,
in that quiet,
even the crickets had gone to sleep,
I'd struggle to recognize the parts of me
that still needed you.
As time and space altered like a never-ending classic,
my furious soul found its calm in the river of solitude,
like I had accepted the wrath of my childhood
in the most graceful way.
Now all there is, is an insensible potion,
that remains static in my throat,
unable to swallow,
neither healing nor aggravating.
I missed having you, my mother.
Time and again.

Complaining to each star my tales of torment,
one certain nightfall,
like the crescent of moon

that unapologetically flaunts its elegance,
I sighed,
and pledged with my undoubting self
to be everything
to my unborn child that you ceased to be for me,
and for that I am indebted.
I Assure you, this is not my agony screaming,
but the silhouette of my waking dream.

Now your memory lies in the scent
of those fish fingers you used to once make,
with your wrinkled hands and your notorious smile,
coming at me with your wooden ladle,
lingering somewhere deep.
Very scarcely pushing its way up,
while having so much to confide,
but not enough room to suffice,
the untouched nude of my love-lorn heart.

But dont you worry,
I've made peace with reality,
as it struck me with patience.
I imagine you gently stroking my untamed hair,
as I ascend to my fantasies,
giggling and spilling teas,
while I break into tears,
and stupidly grumble about my day,
knowing you'll always be there.
I miss your neatly pleated fabric that I'd once adorned;

it carried a warmth that has never been felt ever since.
I fancy your tight embrace,
pacifying a troubled child,
and dwell on conversations we never had.
And wait for a home-cooked meal,
that you so gladly put together,
Making me comfortably numb.

"This above all: to thine own self be true."

– William Shakespeare